Forex Trading

*A Simplified Guide To Maximizing Profits,
Minimizing Losses and How to Use
Fundamental Analysis & Trading Techniques to
Thrive in a Bear and Bull Market*

Penny Stock Trading

If you're interested in getting to know more about trading, there's a preview on one of my other books about Penny Stock Trading at the end of this book called Penny Stocks: *Investors Guide Made Simple – How to Find, Buy, Maximize Profits, and Minimize Losses with Penny Stock Trading.*

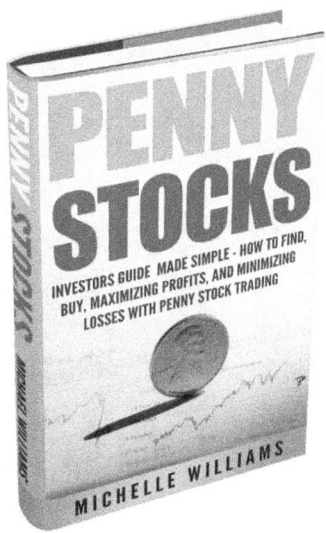

Check out the whole book and others written by me at Amazon.com.

Table of Contents

Introduction

FOREX trading has not lost its luster through the years. In fact, it continues to grow over time expanding its scope of operations to include individual retail investors. If before, foreign currency trading used to be the exclusive turf of the banks whose operational clout were limited to other kinds of financial institutions such as investment firms, pension funds, and hedge funds, it now includes an ever-expanding web of retail FOREX brokers who cater to individual investors.

These retail FOREX brokers continue to draw new individual investors into their folds attracting them with the prospects of making quick fortunes in just a short span of time trading currencies. As a result, retail investors, unmindful of (*or simply ignorant of*) the risks involved in trading currencies continue to pour in their hard earned money into the foreign exchange market– oblivious to the fact that foreign currency trading can cut both ways. It can build you a fortune quickly, or you can lose your shirt just as quick. As per the most recent statistics, about 80% of retail investors lose their initial investments within a short period of time because of this ignorance.

I guess you are one of the many budding investors who have included FOREX trading into your bucket list. Your interest in FOREX trading and your desire not to end up as part of the losing 80%, must have stirred you interest for this book.

Well, let me thank you first for reading this book. Congratulations, because you just discovered the perfect guide to gain a better understanding of the foreign exchange market and a working knowledge on what essentially influences exchange rate fluctuations. You now have the most practical and the most useful trading tool designed to improve your winning chances.

This book, *Forex Trading - A Simplified Guide To Maximizing Profits, Minimizing Losses and How to Use Fundamental Analysis & Trading Techniques to Thrive in a Bear and Bull Market,* is meant to be your ultimate guide in navigating through the stormy waters of the foreign currency market. It will help you reach your investment goals hardly unscathed and possibly brimming with profits. The book presents a candid and lucid presentation of FOREX trading from the retail investor's perspective – totally different from how your brokers have for a long time now made you believe. It gives you a well-informed picture of the foreign exchange market and details of how it exactly operates. It is filled with rich insights which were intentionally hidden from you by your brokers. After going through this book, you will gain a profound understanding of the market and its complex mechanisms thus creating for you a distinctive trading edge.

Thank you once again for reading this book. Happy trading.

Chapter 1

What is FOREX?

FOREX is short for "Foreign Exchange". It refers to money that is denominated in the currency of another nation or group of nations. Because we have different national currencies, exchanging one currency for another became necessary to further international trade and to finance cross-border interactions among nations. It was known as foreign exchange, and it played a crucial role in providing the means by which payments across borders and transferring funds from one country to another are made possible.

This gave birth to the foreign exchange market – a network of foreign currency dealers which serves as the spot market through which all requests or orders for foreign currencies are coursed through and filled. Essentially, it is the foreign exchange market which solely determines the purchasing power of every single currency. The dynamic trading which occurs 24/7 among its participants is geared towards seeking that singularly important price, *the rate of exchange* between currency pairs - the exchange rate is a price reflecting the number of units of one currency that must be surrendered in order to acquire one unit of another currency. This rate moves according to the dictates of existing (*or perceived*) supply and demand levels for one currency compared to another.

Determining the rate of exchange of a currency pair is a highly volatile, continuous process punctuated by frequent wild price swings as the market players progressively adjust their positions shifting from being net sellers to net buyers of the currency in the limelight. Eventually, this rate will finally settle down to a level that is satisfactory to the majority of the market players trading in that particular session. It can be up or down from the previous rate or hardly unchanged depending on the prevailing sentiment that has gripped majority of the market players.

FOREX would not have existed if we lived in a different world which used only a single, common currency. There won't be a foreign exchange market and no foreign exchange rates to worry about since there won't be a need to exchange one currency for another. But since we know this is not the case, we need to understand and grapple with the forces that impact the rates of exchange of various foreign currencies.

You probably may not have put much thought to it, but you have at one time or another engaged in Forex trading yourself. For example, if at a certain point in time you exchanged money in your local currency for money in another country's currency, you have engaged in a legitimate foreign exchange transaction. You have actually traded FOREX. Such transactions involving currencies other than your own is a foreign exchange transaction. Wherever such transactions occur or whatever amount is involved (*be it only a few dollars or billions of dollars*), they are legitimate foreign exchange transactions, and the participants were trading FOREX.

Each of these foreign currency transactions entails a transfer or shift of funds, or any short-term financial claims, from one country and currency to another. It may involve the encashment of a traveler's check overseas by a tourist or funneling millions of dollars into an offshore business acquisition by a foreign investor. It can be a large-scale purchase of foreign currency notes to finance a recently concluded international trade agreement. All these transactions normally involve interbank foreign currency deposits, or other short-term claims redeemable in a currency other than that of the local. Sometimes they are in the form cash or funds available on credit cards and debit cards.

To recap, any transaction involving a currency other than the local currency is deemed as a "foreign exchange transaction." And, in all such transactions, the money almost always is coursed through or flows back into the foreign exchange market - regardless of who are involved in the transaction, or where the transaction occurs, or how much money is involved.

A closer look at the FOREX market will reveal that it is essentially an international network of major foreign exchange dealers each of which is electronically linked with each another. It is so much unlike the stock markets where participants would meet in a well- appointed place to conduct their trading activities. The forex market has no such central location. The participants conduct their trading activities with one another in the comforts of their respective offices (*or even homes*) and simply exchange buy and sell orders electronically. They engage in high-volume trading of foreign currencies around the world via a secured electronic network with order confirmation taking the form of an exchange of bank deposits of different national currency denominations on the outset.

FOREX trading in the late 1990s used to be the exclusive domain of large corporations and financial institutions. The main reason for this is because banks would usually charge small "retail" investors with extremely high transaction costs since they consider their volume as too small to be economically worth their time. However, this rapidly changed sometime in the year 2000 after some prominent broker introduced retail-oriented platforms and started offering online margin brokerage accounts to individual investors. These platforms are capable of streaming prices directly from major banks and from the Electronic Brokering System, which connects to all the major forex market participants. Their idea was to lump together many small trades together and lay them off in the inter-dealer market in larger, aggregate volumes. Because the offered trade sizes are now much larger so much so that formerly adamant foreign exchange dealers were now willing to service the orders from the "retail aggregators" at competitively attractive prices.

Retail FX trading has since grown by leaps and bounds. Data from the 2013 Triennial revealed that retail forex trading accounted for 3.5% of the total forex market turnover and 3.8% of the total spot forex turnover respectively for that year. The largest retail volumes in absolute terms came from the United States and Japan. Japan has the most active retail segment accounting for 10% and 19% of total and spot respectively in April 2013.

The people actively participating in the foreign exchange market are quite a diverse group. Many of them are actually engaged in the "physical goods" market, buying and selling actual merchandise

5

across international borders. Some are venture capitalists who engage in "direct investments" buying plant and equipment overseas. There are also groups of "international portfolio investors" who dabble on overseas stocks and bonds and other financial assets as well as put their funds in international "money market" and short-term debt instruments. There is also this group of investors who are not engaged in trading physical goods much less provide much sought after services. They are there merely to take advantage of price fluctuations speculating for short-term profits that can be had from volatile market conditions.

But, whatever their motives may be in trading foreign currencies, be it for pure investments, or for payment of imports, or to hedge certain business risks related to currency rates, or to create an arbitrage, or simply speculating for profits, or to unduly influence the currency rates (*like the central banks*), they all contribute in significantly tilting the supply and demand equation. By their collective actions, they can move the exchange rates towards a particular direction reflective of current or perceived supply and demand levels.

The incessant interactions among the FOREX market players are both dynamic and synergistic producing a global environment which resulted in the remarkable growth of not only the foreign exchange market but of all the other financial markets as well.

Under such a conducive investment climate, foreign exchange trading began to expand rapidly - progressively developing into a larger and more sophisticated, integrated, and more efficient investment vehicle. If in the past, foreign exchange trading used to be the exclusive turf of the giant banking institutions and a select group of large foreign exchange dealers, the FOREX market has now expanded its scope of operations to include many other kinds of financial and non-financial institutions like investment firms, pension funds, and hedge funds. Its focus has broadened from merely servicing the financial requirements of importers and exporters to handling the vast amounts of overseas investment and other capital flows that currently take place. It has evolved from a series of loosely connected financial centers to a single cohesive international market that plays a direct and far more extensive role in our economies, affecting all aspects of our lives and as well as our prosperity.

Chapter 2

Why Trade FOREX?

Advantages and Disadvantages of Trading Foreign Currencies

Let's face it – FOREX trading has not lost its luster. It continues to draw hordes of individual retail investors into its fold. Despite unverified reports freely floating around that say over 90% of individuals who plowed in their money into FOREX trading lose most if not all of their initial investment, people still continue to put whatever they have saved and stashed away for the rainy days – investing them in the highly volatile and unpredictable forex market.

There could only be one plausible explanation to this – people simply want to grow their money the quickest possible way and apparently trading currencies seems to be the most attractive option for them. It is perfectly normal for people to want to grow their money. The want to preserve the buying power of the money they have saved for the rainy days – money they have worked hard for through the years. They know that the nasty word *'inflation'* has a funny way of slowly chipping away at the buying power of their money making it practically worthless over time. They hope by investing their money in foreign currencies; they will be able to earn enough to offset the diminishing effect of inflation on their net worth.

What is astonishing though is the fact that a great number of these new entrants to the retail forex market are *first-timers* in the field of investments. It is quite surprising why despite the many available and more laid back ways people can invest their money on, these newbies still chose to place their investments on the most volatile financial market in the world – the foreign currency market - where people can lose their shirts overnight. If you don't believe me just look at the ever increasing volume of retail forex trades that remains unabated to this day – an incontrovertible testimonial to this fact.

This may seem whimsical even flimsy for some, but there is a lot of sense to what seems to you as a capricious investment move on their part. But try to think of it, these newbies are investing their money on the biggest and the most liquid financial market in the world. You may not be aware of it, but the foreign exchange market has a daily turnover several times bigger than the combined daily trading volume of *all* the stock markets in the world combined.

That's not all. There are many other advantages in trading foreign currencies compared to other forms of investments which make it more attractive to investors particularly the newbies.

Here are some of them:

No Hidden or Extra Costs. When you trade currencies, you need not worry about brokerage fees, clearing fees, exchange fees, or government fees because there is none. Investors shy away from the stock market, the bond market, or even the money market because there are fees to pay when you place an order and another set of fees when you liquidate.

Minimal Transaction Costs. If you are wondering about out of pocket costs in retail forex trading to tidy up the brokers, there are none. Retail forex brokers don't charge any fee for every transaction coursed through them. If you are wondering how they earn their keep, well, they simply build in their costs on the bid-ask spreads. And, don't worry because it is very minimal. Under normal market conditions, they build in a little less than 0.1%. Some prime dealers even go as low as 0.07%.

24/5 Profit Opportunities. One of the best features of foreign currency trading which attracted traders old and new is the fact that there is always a trading opportunity any time of the day and night. The Forex Market is a 24-hour market operating five days a week. Trading is non-stop commencing on market opening on Monday morning in Australia and ending in the afternoon closing of the bourses on Friday in New York. It is the only financial the forex market that never sleeps. What it means is you will never run out of opportunities to trade and take profits any time of the day or night.

Most Liquid Market. The foreign exchange market has a daily turnover reaching $5 trillion dollars. You can be sure there will always be somebody out there to match your order anytime. You will be able to close out trades instantaneously. There will always be a buyer for every seller and a seller for every buyer. Besides, with that kind of daily trading volume, you can be almost sure that no single entity has that kind of money to unduly influence the market and unduly move prices in their favor. Even the central banks of the Big Four countries (working in concert with one another) miserably failed to sway the prices in their favor several times in the past.

Leverage. With retail forex, you trade with borrowed capital. These are called margin accounts where you are allowed to buy and sell much larger currency contracts than what your actual capital can truly purchase in the spot market. This is called leverage. In the United States, for example, the maximum allowable leverage set bylaw is 50-to-1. It means you can buy or sell currencies worth up to 50 times the money you have currently deposited in your trading account. In other countries, however, it can be as high as 400-to-1. With such a large leverage, investors can maximize their trading capital and allows them to earn hefty profits using very minimal capital.

Low Barriers to Entry. Saving the best for the last, the real reason why more newbie investors flock to foreign currency trading is because it has low barriers to entry. It means with very minimal capital and using only a connected computer, you can start trading currencies online. With as little as $25 you can open a micro account and commence trading immediately. Let's face it, no one can resist the chance to become a trader. Almost everyone is fascinated with the thought of becoming a Wall Street millionaire one day, and the low barriers to entry to foreign currency trading becomes the irresistible gateway to this dream.

Chapter 3

How Much Money Do You Need To Start Trading Forex?

This first question that comes to the mind when one aspires to be a retail forex investor is '*How much money do I need to start trading forex?*' Essentially, the question is meant to determine the minimum amount of capital one needs to put up to be able to open a trading account with a retail forex broker and start trading currencies.

The answer may vary from broker to broker and depends on the type of account you open (*mini, micro, or standard account*). It may range from zero dollars to $1,000. Yes, you are reading it right. There are indeed brokers who will allow you to open zero deposit accounts. Not only that, they will even deposit $25 to $50 of real money into your account for free. There is a catch, though – you need to execute and complete a set number of trades before you can withdraw funds from said account. Clever, indeed. They know based on statistics that 90% of new retail traders lose most if not all of their initial investments and so they are sure they will get back whatever money they may have deposited into their accounts. They have studied the trading habits of newbie traders well, and they know that these traders still lack in knowledge and experience they are likely to commit serious trading blunders. It would just be a matter of time before they end up with zero balance in their accounts. And, this will be long before these newbies can complete the qualifying number of trades before being allowed to withdraw any funds.

Now if you are wondering what motives these brokers have to concoct such an evil ploy on unsuspecting newbie traders, well, it is to get them hooked on forex. You see, forex trading is addictive. Once you've experience that adrenaline rush after you put in that first trade; once you've experienced the thrill and excitement of seeing your account see-sawing from profits to losses - you'll surely get hooked. And win or lose, you will be coming back for more – much like the first time you step inside a casino.

There are micro accounts which you can open with as little as $10. With these accounts, you will be able to trade micro lots, which are equivalent to a mere 1% of a standard lot (or 0.01 of 100,000 of a particular currency). For the standard trading accounts, the minimum initial deposit requirement starts at $200.

Remember, forex trading is done by lots, and one standard lot contains 100,000 units of a particular currency. For example, if you buy one lot of Japanese Yen, you are buying 100,000 Yen. If you buy one micro lot of Yen, you will be buying 1,000 Yen.

However, the real question here is not how much brokers require as initial margin deposit. What you should be concerned with is finding out what would be the ideal amount of starting capital you need to deposit into your trading account so you can trade forex objectively and without pressure. You see, you will be trading on margins, which come with leverage that starts from a low 1:50 (*U.S. brokers only*) to a high 1:500 given by overseas brokers. Now this is an important aspect of forex trading which makes it exceptionally appealing to traders. The high leverage allows you to build a fortune fast using only a small capital – that is, if you happen to be on the right side of the market. But leverage can cut both ways like a double edged sword. You can also lose everything just as fast if you are on the wrong side of the market. Leverage can reduce you to a nervous wreck when the market goes against you as you watch the adverse price movement eating up your trading capital particularly as you near your cut point or margin call point.

So, to answer the real question, the amount of trading capital you should deposit into an account on the onset must be at least three to four times larger than what the broker requires as margin deposit per lot. This should give you sufficient buffer to weather temporary adverse price reactions and buy you enough time to make the necessary adjustments in your losing positions. The rule of thumb being followed by the more experienced traders is limit their exposure on every trade to just 1% of your trading capital. The idea is to make sure you will have sufficient trading capital to initiate new trades to recoup your losses.

The bottom line is the more money you have in your trading account, the farther you are from the risk of getting your positions prematurely cut off during extremely volatile sessions.

Chapter 4

Setting Your Sights with Fundamental Analysis

Fundamental analysis is one of only two methods used by traders to analyze the market with the objective of determining future price movements of a financial asset. (*The other is technical analysis.*) It involves the study of economic, political, and environmental factors as well as other considerations which may profoundly impact the balance between the supply and demand for a particular financial asset. It is essentially an assessment of where or at what price level a specific currency should be trading based on a slew of economic indicators and other important criteria such as seasonal cycles, government monetary policy, etc. In simple terms, fundamental analysis is basically a valuation method to determine the intrinsic value of a currency in relation to other currencies.

The good thing about fundamental analysis is that all reports pertaining to all these important fundamental factors can be accessed by any trader as they are published in real time with relative ease from several online sources - not to mention the exceptional level of transparency that goes with the release these reports. No one gets 'inside information' on what the reports contain prior to their publication. The best part is these reports are released on a regular basis according to a fixed schedule which means you will know what is coming and when. In fact, a forex calendar containing the scheduled releases of the different economic reports together with estimates of market expectation has now become an indispensable tool in every investor's trading arsenal.

It has become the norm to start trading the news prior to their release especially among the day trading aficionados, the big institutional investors, and the market maker brokers who have made such times as an open season for hunting down wayward trades. Indeed, much money has been made (*and much money has been lost as well*) moments before and shortly after the release of some major economic data. Those who made money are those played the market right after anticipating the correct economic data prior to their release.

Quite often, it is the big players who end up making a killing. And, if you are wondering why, the answer is simple – they have a whole retinue of economists cum market analysts whose only job is to sift through voluminous economic data past, present, and future estimates as polled from a number of respected economists) every single minute of their waking hours just to come out with the most probable answers to such questions as:

- Which major country's economy is growing faster than the others? Or, are they growing at all?

- Is the growth healthy and sustainable over a reasonable length of time?

- What are the current monetary policies of each of these countries and the likelihood that there may be changes in the near term particularly with the easing or tightening of credit and interest rates?

- What is the prevailing political condition in each of these countries? (Remember, *Big money runs away from political uncertainties* –if you know what I mean.)

As for individual retail forex traders, it would be next to impossible to do such an extensive analysis of every financial asset's underlying fundamentals – past, present, and future estimates. In fact, they shouldn't. With too much information constantly flooding your consciousness, you are at risk of developing the syndrome called *information overload*. With so much data constantly bombarding your mind (*some of them are even likely to be conflicting*), you tend to be indecisive and get frozen instead of pulling the trigger to get on a trade. With too many variables to consider, you tend to over analyze the market to the point that you paralyze yourself with doubts.

Experienced traders jokingly refer to this condition as *'paralysis by analysis.*

It is enough that you are aware of the implications of the various key economic indicators to the supply/demand and inflation/deflation. It is enough that you understand that the relevance of the actual data that have just been released depends on whether it hits, misses or exceeds the polled consensus of the experts. You should stop short of getting into the shoes of an economist. Instead, you should use your knowledge and awareness of existing fundamentals to uncover the underlying sentiment of the market. Stop trading the news. Start trading the sentiment.

Chapter 5

Temper Your Trades
with Technical Analysis

Technical analysis is a method of predicting price movements and forecasting future market trends based on historical price movements (*past market action*). If the fundamental analysis is concerned with what should happen in the market based on several underlying fundamental factors, technical analysis is focused more on what actually happened in the market. It takes into account only two variables namely the past prices and the corresponding trading volume of a financial asset. It then creates charts reflecting these data and uses it as his primary trading tool to identify commonly occurring chart patterns that serve as the telltale signs indicating if the asset is about to trend or if the current trend is about to end.

One of the basic premises upon which technical analysis is founded is that **prices move in trends**. A trend develops from a strong underlying market sentiment that has taken hold of the market and beholden the majority of the market players who translated the sentiment into actual orders which pushed the price in the particular direction their sentiment dictates. It is this dominant market sentiment which establishes the trend and forms distinctively recognizable chart patterns that reveals whether the underlying psychological state of the market is bullish or bearish.

Market technicians believe that these recognizable chart patterns are recurrent. They will continue to appear in future charts as they had in the past meaning given the same underlying market conditions, traders are likely to trade in the same way as they had in the past. This is the basis of the second premise of technical analysis, and the very reason why traders find it very useful, e.g. **history repeats itself**.

16

Seeing a similar pattern forming on the chart gives the trader a clear idea of where the market is likely to head.

But what really gives substance to the chart based technical analysis is the efficient market theory which says that *the market discounts all and every fundamental underlying a particular asset.* It means anything that can possibly impact the supply/demand equation of a particular currency is taken into account by the market and built in into the price.

If you are keen enough, what you will see in a price chart is the unfolding story of how traders factor into the price every bit of information that can potentially affect the intrinsic value of the financial asset. The peaks and the troughs you see on a price chart signifies the constantly shifting sentiment of the majority as they manifest their market bias by cycling repetitively from bullishness to bearishness and back – over and over again – as new market moving data emerge.

Market technicians find predictive value in the recurring chart patterns. The more creative of them even got encouraged and started to exploit the phenomenon by drafting their own technical analysis models. This resulted in the hundreds of technical analysis tools that we see today all of which are readily available for use by currency traders. The only problem is with so many technical analysis tools to use, traders tend to be more indecisive since many of these tools are often in conflict with one another when it comes to determining where the market is headed. Traders get confused and freeze instead of clicking the button to make a trade. This brings us to our million dollar question – Is there any value in using technical analysis to trade the markets.

The answer to this is simple. Technical analysis is a self-fulfilling prophesy. The more popular technical tools are actually being used by legions of traders who unknowingly end up trading the same asset in unison at practically the same price levels. The sheer number of those who trade the same asset using the same technical tool can unduly influence price movements to a certain degree. For example, there is a possibility that legions of traders are looking at the same level of resistance on a price chart such that as the price rises to this level, many of these traders hesitate to put in more orders while others start to unload – effectively putting a stop to the run up in price. In this sense, the resistance level became self-fulfilling. It is also in this sense that we give importance to the technical recommendations, particularly of the more popular technical analysis tools.

Chapter 6

Working with the Most
Ideal Broker

Individual retail forex traders may not realize it yet, but one of the many reasons most of them lose money is because their own brokers are actually trading against them. According to the latest statistics, 90% of individual retail forex traders lose most if not all of their capital within days after opening their accounts. Brokers who generally cater to retail forex traders are mere retail forex aggregators who merely forward the bulked orders coming from their clients to the liquidity providers who are the real market makers.

The liquidity providers provide their customers with both buy and sell quotations on the various currency pairs in their inventory. You may be unaware of it, but it is perfectly legal for these market maker brokers to be the counter party to the trades entered by their clients. It means every dollar lost by their clients goes to them. If this is not a clear case of conflict of interest, I don't know what is. Unfortunately, this lopsided practice is still being done, and everybody is simply giving it a deaf ear and a blind eye.

Many of today's retail forex brokers particularly those with large order flow volumes do not even forward their clients' orders to the dealing desk of a legitimate market maker broker. With the proprietary trading platforms they give out to their clients, they actually form a small network of their own. They internally match the order of one client with that of another using advanced brokering software. Worst, they act as counterparties to what they deem as losing trades.

It will be wishful thinking to expect that this kind of retail forex brokers will put their client's interest first above their own. It is more logical to expect that they will try to make money not through the usual bid-offer spread (the customary way brokers make money when servicing their clients) but by capitalizing on the trading mistakes of their clients and pocketing their losses.

Why do you think they are able to offer zero bid-offer spreads? Who do you think makes the prices spike every now and then to trigger your trading stops and force you out of the market at a loss? Why do you think slippage occurs and bid-offer spread widens during volatile markets? These are but a few of the manifestations of short-term market manipulations perpetrated by scrupulous retail forex brokers to squeeze the money out of their clients' pockets. The bottom line is retail forex investors enter the market severely handicapped right from the start and hardly aware of it – the very reason why most of them get burned trading the currencies.

The ECN Broker

It is not a hopeless case for the retail forex investors, though. They can dump the retail forex brokers and elect to work with an ECN broker instead (ECN stands for electronic communications network). As the name connotes, an ECN broker is one who uses a sophisticated electronic technology setup to link small clients with tier 1 liquidity providers composed of the major banks and large foreign currency dealers. They don't keep an inventory of currency pairs because they only do order matching – channeling orders coming from small clients directly to the major banks. They charge a fee for every transaction processed, and that's how they make money.

Unfortunately, ECN brokers impose higher initial capital requirement to open an account with them (a minimum of $10.000 initial deposit to start trading). The bulk of the retail forex traders today actually shy away from ECN brokers because of this stiff initial margin requirement. And since retail traders only have minimal capital on hand, they drift towards brokers with whom they can open trading accounts with as low as $50 initial margin requirement. They end up with market makers not realizing that they are getting into a trap where it is impossible to get out unscathed.

Online brokers may be categorized into "Market Makers", "ECN" or Electronics Communication Network Brokers, or "NDD" or No Dealing Desk Brokers. For a neophyte trader, it will be hard to distinguish one from the other. Besides, very few of these online brokers describe their services in detail and more often than not, they make themselves appear as if they are all market makers.

What is a market maker?

A market maker is a broker who provides pricing and liquidity for a particular currency pair and stands ready to buy or sell that currency at the quoted price. The market maker has the volume and the liquidity to take the opposite side of your trade. He has the option of either holding that position or offsetting it partially or fully with the orders coming from other market participants as a way of managing his aggregate exposure to his clients.

Market makers provide both bid and ask prices to customers throughout the day. There are market makers whose quoted prices are "fixed" and remain static throughout the day. Others utilize a dynamic system of determining the spread between the bid and ask prices in real time according to the changes in liquidity of each currency pair.

A market maker will not be able to manage his global foreign currency holdings positions and the entailing risks efficiently unless he collaborates with other market makers and other large market players belonging to the same network including investments banks, Futures Commission Merchants, and other broker/dealers. You will notice too that market makers provide quotes that are slightly different from each other. This is because each of them base their quotes also on their respective current foreign currency exposure as reflected on their individual global FX book.

Essentially, market makers earn their keep via their bid/ask spread revenue, conversions of residual profits or losses, netting revenue, and revenue coming from swap transactions. Their profitability hinges on their ability to manage their respective global foreign currency risks.

A market maker may choose to keep the trader's position without offsetting it with other orders coming from the market. This will mean that the trader's profit is the market maker's loss and vice versa, and may lead to a possible conflict of interest between the trader and his market maker. Please note that a market maker earns from the spread between the bid and ask price and because of this, the trader may at times be at the mercy of the market maker who has the power to increase the spread to minimize his own loss or shave off profits from the traders' position.

What is an NDD broker?

A no-dealing desk broker does not have a dealing desk but instead uses external liquidity providers to provide pricing and liquidity for its clients. The liquidity providers may include banks and other brokers they have networked with. Usually, they have their own proprietary trading platforms which connect to a network of participating banks and other liquidity providers (brokers). The liquidity providers channel their competing bids and offers into the platform, resulting in the best bid and offer being displayed on the client's trading platform.

An NDD broker acts as the pipeline through which orders coming from a customer is passed on to a market maker to be filled at the quoted prices. It is through the broker provided a platform that orders from the customers reach the dealing desk of the market maker for immediate execution at the quoted price. The bid/ask spreads received by the customer are not uniform and may vary depending on which market maker or dealer the orders were routed to by the broker. Some brokers who receive little or no incentive from the market makers are forced to build in their commissions into the spread which explains the variance in the quoted spreads from different brokers.

What is an ECN broker?

ECN is the acronym for the Electronics Communication Network through which large banks, market-maker dealers, and other large financial institutions who are accredited or affiliated to said network funnels their orders for matching and immediate execution.

An ECN broker, therefore, is a broker who is affiliated with or accredited by a well-established ECN network – that's why the name. Unlike a market maker broker, the ECN broker does not have a dealing desk of his own and therefore he does not make or quote prices. What he has which he shares with his clients is a proprietary trading platform which is electronically linked to every market player in the network which includes multiple market makers, banks, and even large individual forex traders. Each one of these market players enter their respective competing bids and offers into the platform regardless of whether said bids and offers are inside or outside the spread. The best bid and offer is then displayed to the trader along with the market book depth and combined available volume at each price.

Under this system, trades are electronically matched. The system may automatically match a trade internally with the bid or offer of another trader. The system also makes it possible for trades to be filled by multiple liquidity providers. It is also possible for a trader to have his buy order filled by liquidity provider "A", and close the same order against liquidity provider "B". All these are possible through the Electronics Communication Network with which the broker is affiliated. Networks of this kind have a wider base of marketplace participants providing pricing which often results to smaller spreads.

And since ECN brokers do not have anything to do with the price quotes much less make them, they try to earn their keep by charging their clients with a small fee for each transaction. Sometimes they are given a rebate by the market makers to whom they funnel in the orders coming from their clients. The amount of rebate given by the market makers depends on the volume of trade or the order flow coming from each broker.

Offhand, it will be difficult to distinguish which broker is of which of the above types since practically everyone is electronically linked with each other and tracing the order flow all the way to the market maker would be a herculean task if not impossible to do. What is more important, however, is to distinguish the legitimate brokers from the sweat shop operators who are there merely to rob you of your hard earned money. On this regards, allow me to point out that the only way you can be sure the broker you are dealing with is legit is to verify his credentials. And, by this, we mean that this broker must be regulated by and answerable to an acceptable, internationally recognized financial regulatory body. It must not be an imaginary, unverifiable entity from some obscure island country in the Pacific.

Chapter 7

Swing Trading Strategy for Retail Forex Traders

One of many reasons why foreign currency trading has remained a shining star to retail forex traders both old and new is because it is highly volatile with frequent (often dizzying) price swings. These traders know that volatile markets provide more opportunities to execute excellent and lucrative trades – that is, as long as they can identify and pick the right *directional changes* in prices as they happen when they happen.

The idea is to catch a changing trend as it is just rearing its nasty head and then ride out this new emerging trend for as long as it last in the direction it is headed. In short, since a trend shifts from an upswing to a downswing or from a downswing to an upswing quite frequently, you will be practically "swinging" from one trade direction to the other quite frequently too.

Some traders have been trying time and again to develop such a trading strategy which they hope would be able to take advantage the price swings resulting from market volatility. They wanted to create an ideal model that can deliver consistent and substantial returns. And, for obvious reasons, they collectively called these strategies as 'swing trading'. Unfortunately, out of the many different swing trading strategies that started to crop up in the past, none was able to deliver the kind of results acceptable to everyone.

The success of any swing trading strategy actually hinges on having a solid and tested method for picking directional changes in the prices. Unfortunately, this is the proverbial 'Holy Grail' of foreign currency trading which for decades now have remained elusive. Everyone has been searching for it albeit without success. Traders could only wish they have such a tool or strategy that can predict shifts in prices before they happen and with a great degree of accuracy. Sadly such does not exist – not just as yet, though. And, in my humble opinion, they won't find it ever simply because they have been looking for it in the wrong direction.

 For one thing, most if not all of the swing trading strategies that have been published so far use one or more of the standard technical analysis tools that have been developed so far - either as a stand-alone tool or in combination with each other - to predict future price directions. Everyone knows that all these technical studies and tools are merely modeled out of or calculated from previous price movements to forecast future price direction – a methodology that has been proven to be ineffective by the huge losses incurred by traders who have been using these strategies.

People tend to forget the fact that the price of any commodity or security is but a reflection of the collective sentiment currently shared by the majority of the players trading in the market at that particular time. For example, if their underlying sentiment about a commodity or security is bullish, then they go on an overwhelming buying spree which pushes the prices up. Conversely, if they are bearish, then they go on a selling spree which pushes the prices down. It is the shift in the sentiment of the majority that we need to be sensitive to since they indicate a possible trend change in the near term.

The problem is - can we measure the underlying sentiment of the majority of the market players at any given time in quantifiable terms? The straightforward answer to this is no. However, we can be immediately alerted to these sentiment shifts with the use of the Japanese Candlestick Charting techniques. With the candlesticks, you can easily discern the strength or weakness of every price move from the length, breadth, and color of every candlestick. They will even tell you when to stay out and remain on the sideline. Amazing, indeed and all you need to do is spend some time to be familiar with candlestick chart formations and the message each of them conveys to you.

Now, here is the best tip for you, if you use the candlesticks along with resistance and support lines you will never get lost - and never guess your way around. Simply pay attention to sentiment shifts that are reflected by the candlesticks formations that occur or coincides with significant support or resistance line – particularly those that pops up –in the level of historical highs or lows. With a great degree of accuracy, the market is likely to either 'hiccup' or take a big leap forward from that point.

The bottom line is there is no better tool to use to formulate profitable swing trade strategy except with candlesticks along with resistance and support lines. So, if you want to be a polished swing trader who can anticipate and take advantage of every price swing, you better beef up your knowledge about the Japanese candlestick charting technique.

Chapter 8

Practical Money Management and Exit Strategies

Most if not all of the retail forex traders today have been lured into putting their money on the line trading currencies in the hope of hitting the Lured into the stormy world of forex trading by the possibility of hitting the 'big one' like George Soros who shorted the British Pound and walked away with a cool $1-billion profit after a single day's trade.

But truth be told, the majority often end up either hitting one big loss or stringing a succession of small losses which drastically impair their invested capital and prevent them from trading any further – with very little chance to recoup their losses. They tend to focus so much on hitting that one big trade chasing the market ceaselessly and getting careless in the process incurring losses which ultimately boot them out of the market for good.

If they only stopped for a while and do some pencil pushing to calculate the implications of their losses to their equity, they probably would have survived long enough to hit the big one. Doing some margin calculations would have made them realize that:

- Losing 25% of their capital on a single trade would require that they achieve 33% return on the next trade merely to restore their equity to the original values;

- Losing 50% would require 100% return on the next trade;

- Losing 75% would require 400% return; and

- Losing 90% would require 1,000% return.

From the above calculations, it is quite clear that recovery can become a herculean task that may even be too tough for the ordinary retail traders to handle. The sad fact is that trading losses are inevitable. Also, the possibility of stringing a succession of losses is also unavoidable. However, what we can avoid is ending up with drastically impaired capital despite stringing a series of losing trades. We can achieve this by having a prudent money management and a practical exit strategy in place.

Money management in forex means controlling the amount of risk capital you put on the line on every single trade including having strategic trading stops in place to limit your losses. Money management strategies can be varied and flexible as the currency market itself but here are some practical tips you can put in place:

- Never risk more than 2% of your account equity on a single trade. Use this to calculate where you should put your trading stops so that you won't lose more than 2% on any trade.

- Put more weight on trading stops that are near or at significant support and resistance lines.

- Implement position sizing when getting into a trade. Here are the rules to follow for position sizing.

Chapter 9

The Importance
of a Forex Calendar

No one can undermine the importance of a *forex calendar* to a foreign currency trader. In fact, every dyed-in-the-wool forex trader cannot do without it. They are always on the lookout for clues on when the market can possibly go ballistics. To them, volatility breeds plenty of trading opportunities. While most conservative traders would normally prefer quieter, more stable markets, hard core forex traders are the exact opposites. They are constantly looking for more volatility in the markets because that is where plenty of profitable trading opportunities can be found. That is why trading the news as they are released (particularly those that impacts the supply and demand balance) has become very much a part of every forex trader's life.

You would be hard put to look for a forex trader who initiates a trade without first consulting his forex calendar. An economic calendar is an indispensable tool and an integral part of every trader's trading arsenal. It contains the schedule of when and at what time various key economic indicators of major countries will be released. What a trader essentially look for on a forex calendar are possible market moving reports that may impact currency price movements profoundly. He constantly tailors his trades around such breaking news announcements in anticipation of a favorable market reaction which can deliver pips to his account fast.

And, since the U.S. Dollar remains the dominant currency to date, traders often gives more weight to and anticipate the release of key economic indicators reflecting the U.S. economy. What adds up to the market volatility is the fact no one really knows what the news will be before they are even announced or published. Ergo, nobody, can really forecast the future price movements with 100% accuracy. And even if anyone knows what the news will be ahead of time, he still wouldn't know how the market will react to it.

Quite often, traders build up positions on both sides of the market as the countdown the announcement of the news begins. Those who believe the upcoming news will negatively impact the market will normally add up more short positions. On the other hand, those who think the forthcoming news will have a positive influence on the market would beef up their longs. Positions start to build up on both sides such that when the news finally arrives, and the market starts heading in one particular direction, those on the wrong side starts running for cover by liquidating positions thus highlighting the particular price movement after the news all the more. In the end, it is the direction chosen by the majority that prevails.

In trading the news, therefore, it is not so much on whether the released report is positive or negative to a particular currency. What matters most is how the majority of the traders view said reports. If trading the news without using the forex calendar would be like trading the market with blindfolds, then trading the market giving mind to the underlying sentiment of the majority would be like jumping out of an airplane without a parachute.

Chapter 10

The Ten Big No-No's
in Forex Trading

1. Know yourself and the market well before you take the plunge.

Trading fast-moving markets such as stocks, currencies, gold, or commodity futures via the internet can be terribly taxing! Before you decide to plunge into it you must know offhand if you are ready to lose a lot of good night sleep for just monitoring the markets; or if you have the stomach to take frequent roller coaster rides during peak market activities (like watching your investment tremendously grow within seconds just to see them melt down in the next!) You must know first if you have the discipline to maintain your cool during wild and wide price swings and still be able to call the shots objectively according to your pre-determined trading objectives. This means you should not to let fear overshadow you when the market moves against your position, nor allow greed to take the better of you when the market is in your favor. Remember always that markets are frequently unpredictable and that you must learn to adapt to its peculiarities fast otherwise, it will eat you up alive.

2. Avoid being scammed. Deal only with registered brokers.

Make sure the broker is registered! If the broker is based in the U.S., contact the Securities and Exchange Commission (SEC) and also check with your state securities regulator as well. You can research the investment online using the SEC's EDGAR database at http://www.sec.gov/edgar.shtml. To contact your state regulator call the North American Securities Administrator's Association (NASAA) at (202) 737-0900 or online at http://www.nasaa.org/home/index.cfm. You may also contact the Commodity Futures Trading Association (CFTC) at http://www.cftc.gov/ and the Financial Industry Regulatory Authority (FINRA) at http://www.finra.org/index.htm. The rule of the thumb you must use here is "avoid the unregistered and junk the brokers with recorded complaints."

For non-US based brokers, you must demand verifiable documentations from the broker regarding their affiliations and representations. Some online brokers are merely introducing brokers (IB), meaning they act as marketing representatives for a bigger broker, in which case you must demand to see the IB contracts and investigate the affiliation of the principal broker. Other brokers "white label" for their principals. Their websites may appear and have the looks of a big broker when in fact they are mere affiliates of other brokers. Don't deal with white labelers if they don't publish their principals. White labelers make money through an additional spread of a pip or two built-in into their price quotes. While I don't have anything against white labelers who are affiliated with established brokers of good standings, I would advise you to avoid them unless they have incorporated more add-on features or services other than those offered by their principals to justify the additional cost to you.

My suggestion is that you deal only with registered brokers is not being biased against overseas brokers. It's just that online investors must always be provided with a forum or a venue to file any claims they may have against their online brokers in the future. And at this point in time, only U.S. based brokers can provide us with this safety net.

3. Never invest money you cannot afford to lose!

One of the major pre-placement considerations an investor must make is determining the amount of capital he will be using. There is not set rule for this. In fact, everything is left to the discretion of the investor. However, one must understand that every investment involves a certain amount of risk. Placing an investment (online or otherwise) is, in reality, a form of risk-taking with the hope that the placement will generate a certain amount of profit after a while.

However, the presence of the entailing risks also tells us that there is a possibility of losses. In fact, in fast moving markets the likelihood of losing all of your investment is all too real. This is the very reason why you must not invest more than your 'risk capital'. Risk capital is that part of your liquid assets or your wealth which if lost will not affect your lifestyle or your family's way of life. Never ever invest money meant for your family's daily subsistence. Doing so will make an emotional wreck out of you. You will turn out to be an emotional trader; setting aside fundamentals; trading out of fear of losing the money on which you and your family depend on; holding on too long to losing positions hoping the market will finally turn into his favor. Once you become an emotional trader, you start trading on false hopes which ultimately lead you to disaster and the total loss of your investment.

4. Use only unprotected computers!

Never access your trading account and other financial records using your laptop in a public place like in an airport, library or an office unless you have a foolproof security system in place. Make sure you only enter confidential information on websites with the "locked padlock" icon in the browser frames (must have https at the beginning of the web address) Avoid using public WIFI facilities in accessing your account or executing your online trades. Hackers are everywhere nowadays. It is advisable to do your online transactions only at the comforts and confidentiality of your abode. Turn off and unplug the computer you are using for trading when you are not on trade.

5. Never execute an order without a trading plan!

Don't trade at all if you don't have a trading plan. A good money manager does not buy or sell out of whims and intuitions. No matter how long his experiences have been in trading a particular market, the successful investor/trader always prepare a plan before taking a plunge, so to speak. His every action stems from a careful study of a particular security, commodity, or currency contract. He always has a sound fundamental basis (underlying economic data) and/or a reliable technical view for the following trading decision parameters:

- the choice of item/market to trade, (which security, commodity, or currency)

- the specific position to take (whether to buy or to sell)

- the specific price range on which the position will be executed (entry point)

- the targeted price objective or exit point on which the trade must be closed

All these trading decision parameters must be clearly defined and set before executing any trade. Never attempt to trade fast moving markets online in the same manner and with the same do or die spirit as in placing bets on online gambling sites. Every trading decision must be based on a trading plan, and every trading plan must be followed to the letter.

6. Use trading stops on every trade!

Every trading plan must incorporate trading stops which shall act as a safety net to limit your losses in case the market moves unfavorably against your established positions. There is no set or fast rule for creating your stops. However, in establishing your initial position you need to set your initial stop with a wider range - taking into account the highs and lows of the trading range established for the day, the proximity of your entry price to historical turn points (chart supports and resistance levels), and your tolerance level as dictated by your initial equity. (Make it a point that your initial stop must not be beyond the price level where it will eat up more than 20% of your equity). When the market starts to move in your favor, adjust your initial stop turning it into a trailing stop in the direction of the price movement. You must adjust your trailing stops tighter and tighter (closer to the spot price) as prices approach historical turn points or significant technical price levels (such as those established using the Fibonacci theory).

Stops are vital to your becoming a disciplined investor. They help you decide without hesitation when to cut a losing or winning trade. They prevent you from becoming an emotional trader and a perpetual loser. But most important of all, trading stops limit your actual losses. I have seen people lose all their investments in one single session because they adamantly held on to losing positions in the hope that the price will soon make a turn-around. I have also seen people who have reached their profit objectives but out of greed, held on to their positions. And when the market whipsawed they ended up losing everything.

7. Never use higher than 250:1 leverage in trading.

One of the main attractions of trading online is the fact that most brokerage houses offer trading opportunities on margin basis (where you are allowed to put up only a fraction of the cost of the contracts you are buying or selling). This ratio may vary from broker to broker. While this is an advantage to the investors since it allows them to maximize the returns on their investments, it can also work against them because high margin ratios can also wipe out their equity fast in very volatile markets. For the more experienced traders who are incorporating strict money management strategies into their trading plans, the margin ratio may be a non-issue. However, for the 'newbies', trading with a lower margin ratio (between 50:1 and 250:1 ratio) will keep them in on volatile markets and allow them ample time to react to rapid price changes in the marketplace. At the same time, the lower margin ratios allow investors to avoid margin calls because it provides them elbow room to make the necessary adjustments on their positions (like temporarily freezing their positions by executing an opposite trade) thus temporarily avoiding actualizing losses. Investors must remember that brokers are not required to issue margin calls when an account falls below the required maintenance margins. They can just go ahead and cut your positions at a loss. Investors need to read, remember, and understand the fine lines in the brokers' agreement regarding margins and margin calls.

8. Do some paper trades first using a demo account before committing actual capital.

Most online brokers offer demo trading on their sites which allow you to open demo accounts and trade live markets using only virtual money. This is a good chance for you to hone up your trading skills in real live market situations without risking your own money. You may do demo trades for as long as necessary (although some online brokers allow you only a maximum of 30 days to use their platform). Never open a real account and put in real money in it unless you already feel comfortable with yourself, your trading plan, the broker's trading platform, and the volatility of the market you are trading. If you are not yet satisfied with the outcome of your initial demo account, then go ahead and request for an extension of the demo account or, better still, open other demo accounts with other online brokers. Do not forget that trading volatile markets require a large amount of self-restraint and discipline so never rush to a decision at all times.

9. Keep abreast of market news at all times. Be sensitive to market sentiment.

You must update yourself with everything that is going on in the financial marketplace. The internet has plenty of sources for real-time financial news updates, commentaries, and forecasts and projections. You must find time to go through the more important items which are relevant to the market you are trading. Do not look only or limit your search to information favoring your current position in the market. You must also be sensitive to contrary news, opinions, and forecasts. Use favorable factual data and information as your basis for initiating your trades. On the other hand, use any contradicting information, opinion or forecast as your basis for setting your trading stops (whether they should be tighter or wider). Subscribe to newsletters from as many online brokers as are available. Most important of all, you must sharpen your skills at digesting all of the available information you happen to go through and be able to create an informed and calculated trading decision from the same as fast as the need arises.

10. Make sure you have a reliable internet connection all the time.

Online investments depend a lot on your uninterrupted internet connections with your broker. Your trading could be adversely affected if for example your internet connection is down at the time the market makes a major move. You can lose a big opportunity to generate profits on that particular market movement, or lose an opportunity to cut your loss if you happen to be on the other side of that market movement. There may also be instances where even the broker's system breaks down due to heavy traffic, or computer glitches, or other natural calamities which may prevent orders from being filled. The online investors must be prepared for such contingencies. They must be familiar with the broker's alternative options in case they cannot access their accounts online. And this should include automated telephone trading, fax orders, and direct phone dealing arrangements. All these alternative trading options must be arranged with your brokers prior to instituting your initial trades.

Conclusion

Thank you again for reading this book!

I hope this book was able to help you to understand foreign currency trading deeper and better particularly how to take advantage of every trading opportunity that crops up as a result of the shifting market sentiment. I also hope you have this book was able to make it clear that the only way to develop a trading edge as a retail forex broker is to further sharpen your knowledge of the foreign currency market from the perspective of a retail forex trader and not limit your knowledge to whatever the brokers feed you and want you to believe.

The next step is to try the concepts you learned from this book and start your way towards your first day of trading towards your first million.

Finally, if you enjoyed this book, then I'd like to ask you for a favor, would you be kind enough to leave a review for this book on Amazon? **It'd be greatly appreciated!**

Feel free to go over to amazon.com and leave a review.

Thank you and good luck,
Michelle Williams

Preview of *Penny Stocks:* Investors Guide Made Simple - How to Find, Buy, Maximizing Profits, And Minimizing Losses With Penny Stock Trading

Introduction

Penny stocks are stocks that cost less than $1. However, the Securities and Exchange Commission defines them as stocks that cost at most $5. There are also financial institutions that have a different cost benchmark in their definition of penny stocks. Therefore, investors must know the benchmarks before they trade penny stocks.

Unlike other investments, penny stocks are ideally for experienced traders only. While it may be true that trading penny stocks can provide significant profits, they can also provide huge losses that can potentially wipe out the hard-earned money of inexperienced traders. As such, new traders must equip themselves with the right information before they can dabble into penny stocks trading.

Fortunately, this book provides the most comprehensive information about penny stocks. By reading this book from cover to cover, a new and inexperienced investor can learn the ins and outs of penny stocks trading before he decides to try it for himself. He has assurance that he does not only learn about the wonderful side of penny stock trading but also the hard truths about it.

This book does not glorify penny stocks investing. It aims to provide the necessary information that a new and inexperienced trader needs to help him decide whether penny stocks trading suits his trading style and financial goals. In the end, it is the hope and desire of the author to educate traders and investors about penny stocks.

Chapter 1:

Introduction to Penny Stock Investing

A penny stock is a type of stock that trades at less than $1 per share. In the United States of America, its Securities and Exchange Commission defined a penny stock as a stock that trades, at most, $5 per share. Despite the price per stock, a penny stock is a very risky investment. As such, even if it trades for more than $5, it is still a called a penny stock.

As it grows, the company needs to increase its cash and resources. Thus, it can decide to offer a penny stock to increase its capital. A penny stock is unpopular because only a few investors invest in it. It does not trade on the regular stock market but on the Over-the-counter Bulletin Board and Pink Sheets. As such, it is important for an investor to be cautious about penny stock trading. While it is true that it can earn huge profits, a penny stock can also cause huge losses.

A penny stock is a risky investment. It is susceptible to pump-and-dump frauds and manipulation. It has low market capitalization and highly volatile. In the United States of America, the Securities and Exchange Commission and the Financial Industry Regulatory Authority issue rules and guidelines for investors who are interested in penny stock investing.

Why Penny Stock Investing is Worrisome

As a thinly traded stock, a penny stock is subject to pump-and-dump schemes by stock promoters and manipulators. More often than not, these unscrupulous people buy a penny stock in bulk. They implement misleading marketing strategies that tend to dupe innocent investors to buy the stock.

If more investors become interested, the price of the penny stock will go up. These unscrupulous people will sell the stock at a very high price to earn a huge profit. The buyers, however, will be holding an empty bag because no one is willing to buy the penny stock. The price will go down and these investors will have to sell the stock at a loss just to dispose of it.

This pump-and-dump scheme takes advantage of fake press releases, chat rooms, email blasts, stock message boards, and websites so that unsuspecting investors become interested in a particular penny stock. In general, a particular individual will claim to have a hot tip and persuade unsuspecting investors to buy a particular penny stock before the price goes up significantly.

When more investors take interest in it, the price will increase so more investors will be encouraged to buy the penny stock. Finally, the unscrupulous individuals will sell the shares and pocket the huge profits. On the other hand, the new stockholders will find it difficult to trade the shares because there are no more interested buyers.

Rapper 50 Cent used the pump-and-dump scheme to increase the price of penny stock HNHI significantly. He had 30 million shares and earned $8.7 million from the transaction. He used Twitter to advertise the penny stock to unsuspecting investors. In another case, Lithium Exploration Group utilized an extensive mail campaign to increase its market capitalization to a minimum of $350 million. It promoted the company even if had no revenues and assets reported in its 10-Q form on December 31, 2010. When the press reported about it, it finally bought lithium exploration assets.

Not only can unscrupulous individuals do a pump-and-dump scheme. A company can use it to promote its stock. If there is momentum, the stock price can move up. However, it is volatile because SEC regulates it. In addition, the spread adds to its volatility. It is possible for the Securities and Exchange Commission to halt trading of a penny stock if it notices a significant rise in the price quickly. Investors cannot control their shares when the SEC approves trading again.

How to Regulate Penny Stock Trading

A penny stock has to meet some standards before anyone can trade it. In the US, it must have a price, minimum shareholder equity, and market capitalization. If it trades on the stock exchange, the stock, referred to as low-priced, is not a penny stock even if it trades below $5.

The SEC and the FINRA control trading of penny stock. In the State of Georgia, trading of penny stock has to follow its comprehensive penny stock law. The US regulators like FINRA and SEC revised their regulations in order to restrict brokers and dealers effectively. However, it is still possible for unscrupulous groups and individuals to implement pump-and-dump strategies.

Chapter 2:

Risks and Potential
of Penny Stocks Trading

Penny stock trading is very risky. However, it is possible for an investor to earn significant returns from it. Many people have also lost a lot of money from it. Many companies that are on the verge of bankruptcy often offer penny stocks. There are scammers who use shell companies to entice unsuspecting investors to invest in penny stocks. In addition, these corporations are often overleveraged.

Penny Stock Investing Risks

Trading of penny stocks occurs through the Pink Sheets or Over-the-Counter Bulletin Board. If he wants to invest in a particular stock, an investor will have a hard time researching for information about the company so he may not be able to make a logical decision. Furthermore, sources are not credible. In fact, both exchanges have no standards for a company to meet before it becomes part of either Over-the-Counter Bulletin Board or Pink Sheets.

In addition, investors can easily buy a penny stock, but they may find it difficult to sell it, especially if they want to lock in their profits. There are few investors who are interested in penny stock investing. Thus, these investors may have to sell their shares at a lower price or wait for interested buyers. If they decide to wait for willing buyer, they trap themselves in a pump-and-dump scheme and eventually lose their money. If they decide to sell at a lower price, they will realize a reduction in their profits.

There are also many unscrupulous groups and individuals who offer "hot tips" about a specific penny stock. An unsuspecting investor may receive email blasts or brochures through snail mail. Usually, these materials contain outrageous claims about the stock making significant gains because of its modern technology. The investor has no knowledge about the company or people sending him the information. He is not aware that the source of information is actually just trying to sell his shares at discounted prices.

The Penny Stock Possibilities

An investor must cease the pump-and-dump strategy if he wants to earn from a penny stock. He has to buy the penny stock the moment he receives the junk mail then wait for other people to buy it. Then, he quickly sells his shares to lock in his small profits. In penny stock investing, timing is important. The investor cannot miss the initial surge in trading volume because he will lose money if he does.

The investor can also make a research on penny stocks. He needs to perform due diligence and study the companies' fundamentals. He can check their corporate websites for information. He has to study their balance sheet to ensure that these companies do not have many debts. The companies must be profitable or are able to reduce their losses.

The Risks of Penny Stock Investing

The investing public has no means to get all information. A wise investor needs to perform due diligence before he invests in money. However, the Securities and Exchange Commission do not regulate stocks on Pink Sheets so the investor may find it difficult to search for credible information about the penny stocks.

Companies do not need to meet some standard requirements before they can list their stocks on Over-the-Counter Bulletin Board and Pink Sheets. There are companies that do not meet the minimum standard requirements of the major exchanges so they list their stocks on Pink Sheets and Over-the-Counter Bulletin Board. Although Pink Sheets does not have requirements, the Over-the-Counter Bulletin Board requires companies to file documents with SEC on a timely manner.

Companies, listed on Pink Sheets and Over-the-Counter Bulletin Board, are either new companies or nearing bankruptcy. As such, they have no record of accomplishment. An investor will find it difficult to assess the penny stock potential if the company cannot profit any proof of good performance.

Lastly, penny stocks are illiquid. This means that an investor may not be able to sell his shares because only a few buyers are interested. The investor can opt to sell them at a lower price if he wants to dispose of them immediately. In addition, some groups and individuals may use pump-and-dump schemes to manipulate the penny stock price.

Penny Stock Scams

It's not only investors who have problems with a penny stock. Even the SEC also sees penny stocks as problematic because this kind of stock is often a target of scammers due to the penny stock's poor liquidity and companies' tendency to provide little information.

There are companies that employ unscrupulous means to encourage investors to invest in them. They pay other companies and individuals to recommend their penny stock through the different media like newsletters, radio shows, and financial programs on television. An unsuspecting investor can also receive spam emails about how a particular penny stock can be a great investing opportunity. It is best for this investor to determine if these people or companies recommending the penny stock are paid or not.

There are also offshore brokers who dupe possible investors. The SEC can allow companies to sell their stock to offshore investors without the need to register the shares with the government regulator. However, some companies sell their shares at a discounted price to foreign investors. In return, these investors sell back the shares to US investors at a higher price. The SEC does not allow this kind of transaction.

Misconception about Penny Stock

There are people who spread wrong information that some of the most popular stocks began as penny stocks. They want unsuspecting investors to believe that these large companies started small and their stocks increased in value. However, a diligent investor will find out that the price of the stock of companies like Microsoft and Wal-Mart became pennies due to stock splits. Actually, these corporations offered their stock to the public at a high price.

Many investors invest in penny stocks because they thought that these investments would increase in value and provide opportunities for their wealth to grow. For instance, an investor buys a particular penny stock for $0.10 per share. If the share price increases by $0.05, he makes a 50% profit. Therefore, his $1,000 initial investment will become $1,500. However, he fails to realize that he can also lose $500. Worst of all, he can lose his entire capital.

You can find and check out the rest of the book on Amazon.com

Other books written by me

(You can check them out at Amazon.com)

- **Penny Stocks:** *Investors Guide Made Simple – How to Find, Buy, Maximize Profits, and Minimize Losses with Penny Stock Trading*

- **Dropshipping:** *The Ultimate Dropshipping BLUEPRINT Made Simple - Find, Launch, And Sell Your First Private-Label Product*

- **Etsy:** *The Ultimate Guide Made Simple for Entrepreneurs to Start Their Handmade Business and Grow To an Etsy Empire*